Spring

Arrangements
from the
Southern Garden

Spring
Arrangements
from the
Southern Garden

Floral Design and Text by
Ralph Null

Photography by
Greg Campbell

Harmony House Publishers

Acknowledgments

The author would like to thank all those who have assisted and given me the encouragement and assistance to do this project. My special thanks to Fred Kinder and Walter McKay who provided direction with the formatting and editing. I am also grateful to Barbara Hodges, Meredith Kinsey, Charlie and Janice Bond, Joni Miller, Elizabeth Kaye, Pat Kaye, and Pat Crouse for generously sharing the flowers and foliages from their homes. A special thanks to Pam Smith at Nature's Flowers, as well as Paul Smith and Bill Taylor. Greg Campbell's willingness to try something different improved the photography selections. And especially William Box who opened his home for many of these settings.

Harmony House Publishers - Louisville
P.O. Box 90 Prospect Kentucky 40059
502.228.2010
©2001 Ralph Null
All rights reserved
Printed in Hong Kong
Executive Editor - William Strode
Design - Karen Boone
Library of Congress Control Number: 2001089872
ISBN 1-56469-083-0

Contents

$\mathcal{T}$he Southern garden can evoke many ideas. There are those who would envision the lush gardens and plantings around the classical columned homes of the old South while others might be more inclined to think of country farm houses with traditional landscapes and planted vegetable gardens. Others might see the contemporary landscaped, clipped and trimmed yards of today's subdivisions. Whatever you think of when you hear Southern garden, it would probably fit somewhere in between each of these. The South is rich in its landscaping and gardening heritage. The yard or garden has always been an important social statement that reflects the care and desires of the homeowner.

I'm inclined to think of all of these myself. Everything from the old fashioned swept yard of an elderly neighbor from my childhood to the elegant city homes with rolling lawns, dramatic foundation plantings and borders which might include roses, annuals, and perennial cutting gardens. The most important aspect of this is the diversity and adaptability of the plants chosen for the garden. Sharing "pass along" plants, bulbs, and cuttings has long been a fundamental part of what makes a Southern garden special. Many areas of the South are very rural and pastoral. Some of my favorite areas of collection will often extend into the woodlands, along the country roadsides, the pastures, and the fence borders where pickings are often "exotic" and exciting.

In choosing foliage and flowers for this book, I have looked for those items that were available and plentiful. Yet, sometimes it only takes one or two blooms or a branch to set the right mood in a design. One of the characteristics of the Southern style is the inclusion of diverse foliages and branches. Whether this comes from the need to create designs that are large and lush to fit the large scale traditional home or the need to bring to the indoors part of the natural environment, I am not sure. But I do know that this helps to give a definite style to the arrangements. Even the addition of only a few stems of garden foliage can make a bunch of market flowers seem to be much more natural and garden like.

Sharing with friends from the garden is sometimes the best part. I'm particularly thankful to friends and neighbors who so frequently, knowingly and unknowingly, have contributed to my garden arrangements including those in this book. One of the joys of small-town living is the ability to know who has what blooming in their garden, or what special foliage they grow, or best of all to know that they enjoy sharing with others who also like doing flower arrangements.

As you read this book and look at the designs, you will see that many are very small. But what could be more beautiful than a tiny glass of a hundred violets? Other designs are large and full of many kinds of flowers. Perhaps what I would most like to share in this book is that there are many places and ways to use flowers in the home. Flowers help to make any occasion special, and any placement extraordinary. At the end you will see flowers used in the most beautiful place of all, the altar of the church.

I hope that this book will bring you pleasure and enjoyment as you look at the pictures. Maybe a pleasant memory of times past will come. But most of all, enjoy the flowers.

For Entertaining

A corncob basket filled with amaryllis, anemones, azalea,viburnum, Queen Ann's lace, and woodland hyacinths echo the spirit of spring.

This mass arrangement

is made of larkspur, jasmine,

miniature Amaryllis, lilies,

privet, dianthus, bells of

Ireland, alstroemeria, and

Scotchbroom. It creates

a dramatic accent in the

foyer of the home.

Even tea for two can be a grand affair when the table is decorated with beautiful garden spirea, viburnum, and azalea.

*C*andlelight
and early spring
climbing rose
blossoms create an
eloquent setting.

*C*amellias
and strawberries
make a great
welcome to
spring.

The spring branches of blooming buck-eye are "country casual."

This basket of spring vegetables, accented with blooming kale and Joe Pye weed, brightens the kitchen.

The simplicity of a frosted glass vase filled with Queen Ann's Lace is beautiful.

Honeysuckle and hydrangea capture both beauty and fragrance.

Small & Simple

When you take a walk in the garden, stop and pick a few blossoms of whatever is blooming. Arrange them for your table. Their bright colors and fragrance will restore your faith that winter is leaving and spring is awakening.

Sometimes we only need a simple touch.

All of these blossoms are from the pots by the kitchen door. Just ones and twos of things make beautiful arrangements.

The illusion can be half the fun! These parrot tulips have been arranged in a crystal bowl centered with a crystal ball.

The painted faces of pansies are fun and carefree, but their fragrance is a touch of heaven.

*A*ssorted foliages, green and variegated, make spectacular designs.

*W*hat could be more spring-like than a collection of bunnies playing around a vine basket filled with pastel colors, mint, ivy and a few pansies?

*Mother never
let me go barefoot
until I could pick
a bouquet of violets
at the railroad
trestle. Finally
spring is here and
my feet are free!*

$\mathcal{N}$aturally Growing

It's great fun to create a design that recreates a little spot from the garden. This large ceramic plate is encircled with a wreath made of honeysuckle vines. The center is filled with amaryllis, blackberry branches, Solomon's seal, mock orange and moss. Birds and nests complete the naturalistic, botanically styled design.

*H*yacinths and
muscari dropped
into crystal vases
are so easy and
most effective.

This driftwood styled ceramic container is the perfect choice for these few stems of Louisiana iris, narcissus and mint.

This illusion of a growing garden was created by using red onions as the lily bulbs. The stems of the lilies are inserted through the onions and into the wet floral foam hidden under fresh moss.

Nothing compares with a few tulips "growing" in a special place.

Capture the feeling of natural growth by arranging the flowers as if they are planted.

$\mathcal{L}$ush
& Romantic

*The eloquence
of this arrangement
of iris, narcissus
and honeysuckle is
enhanced with the
antique Georgian
epergne and plateau.*

This vase of dried birch and pussy willow branches has been brought to "life" by adding Dutch iris.

Branches of kerria, forsythia, viburnum, azalea, and tulips create a dramatic mood in this antique coffee server.

*L*ush unusual combinations, on a grand scale, are dramatic and fun to create.

*W*hat says spring more loudly than massive bouquets of azaleas and tulips.

For a long lasting arrangement, gather branches of photinia, redbud, and native azalea and let them go from bud to bloom in the vase.

Wait until spring to prune flowering shrubs and trees. Enjoy the prunings as in this vase of dogwood and azalea.

From the Market

A touch of garden foliage can work magic with a market bunch.

*A*dding
garden foliage
and a few early
blossoms to a
market bunch
gives the illusion
that it's all
from the garden.

*S*ometimes
spring is just
color. When
nothing is
blooming in
the garden, a
market bunch
of flowers can
fill the need
for a cheerful
touch.

A market
bunch of roses and
a bag of lemons
create a dramatic
look. Arrangements
raised off the table
create more impact.

$\mathcal{A}$
Garden Party

Vertical arrangements create dramatic and strong visual accents.

Candlelight helps set the mood for a spring garden party.

Interesting containers can be the key to exciting centerpieces.

Romantic Wedding

ridemaids' Bouquets of dusty miller, hydrangea, and hosta "garland" these cupids for decoration following the ceremony.

The bouquet for the bride is made of hydrangea, lily of the valley and running roses. The mother's posies feature garden flowers.

Nothing is more lovely than the radiant beauty of peonies, hydrangea, Queen Ann's lace and ivy in a lush massive arrangement.

*F*lowers for
worship speak
to the soul and
fill the heart
with joy.

*I*n the church
the wedding pew
is festooned with
a hand-tied
bouquet of roses,
hydrangea,
Queen Ann's
lace, and ivy.

onclusion

Take time to stroll the garden. Smell the roses,

and look at all the beauty that surrounds you.

Whether your garden is only a pot on your

window sill or many rolling acres, enjoy it.

Gather a flower and admire its beauty. Share it

with a friend or stranger. You will be amazed

at the power of a few blooms to lift the spirit,

to create a smile, or to make a friend for life.

Enjoy!